The carved pataka store houses, for safe keeping of prized items and of food, had their own tekoteko on the high part of the roof. Other supplies, particularly of kumara and water, were stored in underground pits or rua.

The tuwatawata palisade was made of totara, puriri, or hinau timber or heart of kowhai, all stout, strong trees.

Whare puni, the thatched sleeping houses, were often dug down into the earth for greater warmth.

Date Due

| L.W. | | | |
|---|---|---|---|
| MAR 0 2 2005 | | | |
| | | | |
| | | | |
| | | | |
| | | | |
| | | | |
| | | | |
| | | | |
| | | | |
| | | | |
| | | | |

## THE HOME OF THE WINDS

This new book completes the trilogy which started with *The House of the People*[1], and was followed by *The Fish of Our Fathers*[2]. The first book won the Russell Clark award for the most distinguished illustrations in a children's book; the second won for both author and artist the prestigious N.Z. Children's Picture Story Book of the Year Award for 1985. The judges called it 'an outstanding book'.

THE HOME OF THE WINDS describes and illustrates the building and fortification of a pa on a site chosen for its defensibility. The ancient lore of the Maori people, their beliefs and skills, their affinity with nature are revealed in an authentic tale of pre-European days.

[1] *The House of the People* describes the building of a meeting house, and
[2] *The Fish of Our Fathers* the construction of a war canoe.

### About the Author

Ron Bacon, Australian by birth but New Zealander by habit and long time residence, has written two adult novels, two books in co-operation with photographer Greg Riethmaier on their adopted city of Auckland, as well as several children's books, two in collaboration with artist Para Matchitt.
Married with three children, he is now Principal of a South Auckland primary school.

### About the Artist

Robert Jahnke, a graduate of the Elam School of Fine Arts, Auckland, and the California Institute of the Arts, is an art teacher at Mangere College. He is married, with one child.

# The Home of the Winds

Story by R.L. Bacon

Illustrations by R.H.G. Jahnke

Published by Child's Play (International) Ltd 1986

085953-302-6

First published 1986
Waiatarua Publishing
P.O. Box 87003, Meadowbank
Auckland 5

Text © 1986 Waiatarua Publishing
Illustrations © 1986 Waiatarua Publishing

Typeset by Auckland TypoGraphic Services Ltd.
Printed in Singapore

First Published in Great Britain 1986
by Child's Play (International) Ltd.
ISBN 0-85953-302-6

## Glossary

Many of the Maori words in our story are explained by the story itself, but here are some words which may need further explanation:

heketua - a latrine, a place for disposal of rubbish.

kainga - a village, a collection of houses.

marae - the open place in a village, a gathering place for the people, but more than this, the marae is the spiritual home-place for each Maori.

mokopuna - grandchildren.

pa - a fortified village.

Papa - in Maori mythology, the Earth Mother.

piupiu - a skirt-like garment.

poi - a tightly rolled ball of New Zealand flax on a plaited string, an important rhythmical adjunct to women's dance.

Rangi - in Maori mythology, god of the sky, the Sky Father.

taiaha - the Maori warrior's long fighting club.

Tane - god of the forest and all living things of the forest.

Tawhiri-matea - god of the winds.

Te Poho o Rua - The Body of Rua.

tohunga - the experts of the kainga, those wise in the ways of carving, of fishing, of patterning in kowhaiwhai painting, wise in all the lore of the Maori.

tuna - New Zealand's freshwater eel.

whare puni - a sleeping house.

whare whakairo - a superior carved house. (One house or many, it is still whare, not whares. Other words like this, which may mean one or many, are taiaha (long club/s), kainga (village/s), tuna (eel/s). Look at words such as these, and decide, when they are used in the story, whether they refer to one or more than one.)

These are very brief explanations; in many cases the full and true meaning of a Maori word, with its deep spiritual and emotional quality, cannot be expressed briefly or adequately in English. Dialect, location, tribal differences, all have an effect on meaning; our explanations refer to the use of the word in our story.

## Pronunciation Key

Pronounce a as in art.
e as in pet.
i as ee in feet.
o as in for.
u as oo in too.
wh as f in fat.
ng as ng in sing.

Pronounce each vowel separately and always with the same sound, although vowel length may vary.

## Page numbers

Wherever possible we have numbered the pages with the hindu-arabic numerals which you all know. In addition we show the Maori words for these numerals. On some of the pages, where the illustration covers the area completely, the page numbers have been left out. These numbers, with the Maori equivalent, are shown below.

11 (tekau ma tahi)
12 (tekau ma rua)
21 (rua tekau ma tahi)
26 (rua tekau ma ono)
27 (rua tekau ma whitu)
28 (rua tekau ma waru)
29 (rua tekau ma iwa)
30 (toru tekau)
31 (toru tekau ma tahi)

There was a time, my mokopuna, a time long ago when the people lived on the shores of a wide blue bay. The soft winds of Tawhiri-matea blew over the bay. Ika-moana the fish, ika-moana the children of Moana the sea, swam in its waters. In the forests and swamps near the kainga were many birds, and all over the bay and the kainga, Ra the sun shone warm and bright.

There came a day when the rangatira, the chief of men, said to the oldest tohunga, "Come, listen to me and talk with me. I say to you, this place where we live is a good place to live. Ra the sun shines on us, many birds fly in the forest, there are many eels in the swamp.

"Our people have many good things. We have many fine cloaks from the skin of kuri the dog, many soft cloaks from the feathers of kiwi and kereru the pigeon. Out in the bay, ika-moana the fish jump and swim. There are birds in the forest, the fern grows high on the hills. Everywhere there is plenty of everything for everyone."

And the oldest tohunga said, "Ae, truly this place where we live is a good place to live."

"But hear me," said the rangatira. "Hear what I say. We must take care that enemies do not come. Enemies may see our bay. They may see our forests where our birds fly, may see our swamps where our fat tuna swim. Enemies may come and try to take from us our lands and all our other good things."

And the oldest tohunga said, "Ae, truly this kainga is a good kainga. But it is not a good place for us to be if we must fight our foes. We must build for us a pa, a strong pa high on a hill, a hill so high that it will be hard for enemies to come near."

"Come then," said the rangatira. "Let us hold a hui. We will call the people to a hui and tell the people of the kainga the things they must do."

So the rangatira and the tohunga called the people and spoke to the people and the people listened and they said, "Ae, we have listened and we have heard. We have heard the things you say and what you say is good to hear. Ae, we will build such a pa."

So all the people went to a high place near the bay.

And from the high place they looked to a hill by the bay and the oldest tohunga said, "There, on that hill, is a good place for us to live. So high is that hill that it comes near the home of the sky father, Rangi. There we will see if enemies come in canoes from across the bay. We can watch if they come from the hills far away. There we will be able to see if enemies come to take our lands."

And from the high place, the rangatira and the oldest tohunga and all the

people stood, looking. And the tohunga said, "Ae, I see that hill as a good place for our pa. I see, there on the side of the hill, where Ra the sun shines bright and warm, there I see our gardens will be. There our men will chant and sing and dig the warm brown soil with their ko sticks. There our women will kneel to plant the red-brown kumara. There, from our gardens, we will take the kumara and store them for the long cold winter, store them in pits dug in the soil of the hill."

"There are trees there too, near where our gardens will be, trees where our hunters may spear the birds and snare the birds, spear the children of Tane to use as food for the winter. Ae," said the rangatira, "that hill is a good hill. There, on that high hill, we will build our pa."

And all the people shouted, "Ae, it is good. There, on that hill by the bay, we will build our pa."

**9**

iwa

Then the rangatira said, "For our pa to be strong, we must build round it a fence. Ae, we must make a fence, a tuwata-wata of hinau tree, a fence strong and tall so no enemies can climb over. But under the first corner post of the tuwatawata, place there the mauri stone that will be the life-place of our pa, the mauri stone to be the place where the gods live in our pa. And dig a ditch, deep and wide, outside the fence so no enemies can jump over.

"And at the waha-roa of the pa, at the coming in place of the pa, make and carve a gate piece for the pa, a gate carved from the warm red wood of totara, to welcome friends when they come, but strong to keep out foes. Now, at the corners of the pa, build taumaihi, taumaihi strong and high so our warriors may climb there and watch out over the swamps and the bay to see who comes. Ae," said the ranga-tira, "let these things be done."

And the people said to the rangatira, "All these things we will do."

**10**

tekau

"Now," the rangatira said, "inside the tuwatawata, make for the people whare-puni, whare-puni of raupo reeds tied with supplejack and vine. And dig the floor of the whare-puni down into the warm earth, so Papa the earth mother may hold the people warm and safe, so the winds of Tawhiri-matea may not blow through, so the people may stay safe and warm as they sleep."

And the people said once more, "Ae, we hear. All these things we will do when we build our pa."

Then the rangatira said, "And we must build pataka, pataka to keep safe our tiki and cloaks and other good things. Build the pataka on tall poles so kiore the rat and kuri the dog may not get in. But make a ladder, an arawhata of rimu wood that men may climb to bring food down from the pataka. But after, take the arawhata down, take it away, so kuri or kiore cannot climb too!

"Then, go to the bay, catch ika-moana the fish, the children of Moana the sea. Catch the fish and dry the fish in the warmth of Ra the sun, and put the fish in the pataka so we may have food when the winds of Tawhiri-matea lash the seas to foam. And birds in gourds of fat, and kiore too, put them in the pataka for food. Then, if enemies come, there will be food in the pataka of the pa so the people may eat.

**13**

tekau ma toru

"And in our pa, in the wide open place of the pa, we will make a marae. A marae great and wide where our warriors may practise the haka, stamp their feet and shake their taiaha and set their hands a-quiver and shout their awful shout so enemies will fear to come.

"A marae where our maidens may sing their songs and slap their poi and clap their poi on hand and thigh.

**15**
tekau ma rima

"A marae where our mokopuna may play their games, catch their knuckle stones, spin their tops, and throw their darts of toetoe grass.

**16**
tekau ma ono

"A marae where our women may tend the cooking fires, bake the fern root and berries of karaka and tawa, cook kumara and kiwi and kiore, cook food to make our warriors strong, food to make our moko-puna grow into fierce fighters and proud wahine.

**17**

tekau ma whitu

"Ae, and when our friends from places far off and away know that we have built this fine pa, they will come to see the pa we have made. They will bring gifts and food to show they are our friends. Ae, we

**18**
tekau ma waru

must make our marae wide for when friends and
visitors come. Make it wide and make it fine so many
people may come, sit with us, and talk with us and be
with us on our marae."

Then the oldest tohunga said, "And by the marae, looking to the marae, we will build a mighty whare-whakairo, a whare-whakairo so large and so fine that all the people from far and near will know that this, our whare-whakairo, is the finest house in all the land.

"Build our house tall and build our house strong, tall as our ancestor Rua was tall, strong as Rua was strong.

"And we will call our house Te Poho o Rua so all the people in all the land will know that it is as if our ancestor Rua, Rua who has long gone to the spirit land, as if Rua has come back to be with us once more.

"Come then," said the oldest tohunga, "come, go with me to the forest of Tane. There, in the forest, I will speak with Tane and ask Tane if we may take trees from his forest. From the forest we will need a tree, a tree straight and tall to be the tahuhu of our house. Ae, a tahuhu to be the roofpole of our house, to be the strong backbone of our house, even as our ancestor Rua was strong.

"Now, for the front of our house," the oldest tohunga said, "for the front of our house, carve maihi, mighty maihi to stretch down like arms from the front roof of the house, to hold our people and to welcome our people when they come to the house.

"And from the forest," the oldest tohunga said, "we will cut trees to be the poupou of the house, cut mighty slabs of totara tree to make poupou to hold high the rafters of the house, poupou to make strong the sides of the whare-whakairo.

"We will carve the poupou with staring eyes of paua shell, with out-thrust tongue, with teeth, with toes, with mere in hand. Carve the poupou to be fierce when the fire flame flickers in the whare-whakairo, fierce to watch the people and keep them safe in our house, Te Poho o Rua.

"And when we have done these things," the oldest tohunga said, "we will go again to the forest of Tane, to cut trees once more, trees to be the rafters of our house, the heke of our house, the ribs of our house, heke to hold the roof of the house high above the people in the house. And when the heke are high in the roof of the house, then you must go in your canoes out over the bay. Take your strongest lines and your strongest hooks and catch mango the shark. From the oil of mango, from soot of fires, from red clay of Papa, you must make paint to paint the heke of the house in kowhaiwhai swirl of black and white and red. Paint the curling, swirling waves of sea, paint the patterns of forest and fern. Ae, paint the heke of our house so our house will truly be a fine house."

**23**

rua tekau ma toru

And the oldest tohunga spoke to the wahine, to the women of the kainga, saying, "Now is time for you, the women, to weave tukutuku for the walls of our house Te Poho o Rua. Ae, weave tukutuku of flax and of reeds, tukutuku to go between the poupou of the walls, to make warm the walls, when the winds of Tawhiri-matea blow round the house in winter. Ae, of poupou and of tukutuku we will make the walls of our house so our house will be warm when winds of winter blow."

Then the oldest tohunga spoke to the tohunga of carving, saying, "Now, you carving men, carve tekoteko for the front high place of the house, a tekoteko to look out over the marae, to keep safe the people in our whare-whakairo, a tekoteko to watch that no harm comes to those who live on our marae.

"Do these things," the oldest tohunga said, "build our house and carve our house and make our house a fine house where people may come and talk and meet. Make our house Te Poho o Rua a mighty house even as our ancestor Rua was a mighty warrior, even as our pa will make us a mighty people, feared by our foes."

And the rangatira said to the oldest tohunga, "Ae, you have spoken well." And to the people the rangatira said, "Let these things be done. Do these things so our pa will truly be a fine pa. But other things we must do. There, where the cliff is steep and high, there you must build the heketua, so the rubbish and the waste of the pa and of men may be cast down the cliff and be gone for ever.

"And you must build a path down the hill so our fisher folk may go down the hill to their canoes, to take their canoes out over the bay to catch ika-moana, ika-moana the fish, children of Moana the sea.

"And our women may use the path too, use it when they go to the swamps to cut flax, use it when they go to the swamps to soak the flax for piupiu, to colour and to dye the flax for piupiu in the soft black mud of the swamp."

And all the people listened to hear the rangatira and the tohunga speak, and the people cried out, "We hear what you say. All the things you say are good things to hear. Ae, these things we will do. We will make our pa a good pa, a strong pa, a mighty pa, a pa where we may be safe from our foes."

Then the people began to do the things to build the pa.

Long did they work and hard did they work until the work was done.

And when the work was done, the rangatira and the tohunga and all the people looked on their pa, and they said, "Ae, it is good. Our pa where we will live is done. High on this hill we will live, high near the home of Rangi, high where the winds of Tawhiri blow."

And the rangatira said, "Ae, I feel the winds of Tawhiri blow. I feel their touch, I see them go through the grasses. So high is our pa on this hill, this must surely be the place where the weary winds come for rest. Ae, I will name our pa Te Turangawaewae o Tawhiri so all men from all over our land will know that this pa where we live is truly Te Turangawaewae, is truly The Resting Place, is truly The Home of the Winds."

The stronger posts of the tuwa-tawata were the pou turangi. Pou turangi tops would often be carved as tekoteko, or fierce figures, named after male ancestors.

Taumaihi was one of the names for the tall towers where war-riors kept watch for enemies. Rocks and stones were kept on the platforms of taumaihi, ready to be thrown down at enemies.

A pa might have three or four rows of palisade fence. The main row was the tuwatawata.

At the main entrance to the pa, at the waharoa, stood the tall carved gate piece.